The Pain Boxes:
Healing and Letting Go

Aura Garden

BookLeaf Publishing
India | USA | UK

Presentation by *BookLeaf Publishing*

Web: www.bookleafpub.com

E-mail: info@bookleafpub.com

ISBN: 9789357215558

First edition 2022

To all who see me, accept me and love me as I am.

Anxiety

Anxiety
Bitter enemy
I resist
A pulsing chest
A stomach wrench
My words falter
My being alters

Anxiety
Sweet part of me
I do not resist
A throbbing chest
I take a breath
You hold my hand
Only together
Can we make our stand

Failure

There is nothing quite like
The doom of failure
To know I tried
With everything I had
And to still

Come up short

To accept I have nothing left
To offer
And what I had
Was not enough

There is nothing quite like
Finding a place
I don't have to try
To just get by

To be seen for what I am
To fly
To always be
Enough

Violated

I didn't see your face
But I felt your hands
In that special place

Violated
My trust in others
Annihilated
My personal space
Deconsecrated

I should always get to choose
Who can touch me
And who to lose

And for the one I chose
Thank you
For giving me the space
To be alone
Until I was ready
To welcome you home

Broken

You don't remember it
But I do
You said, "Shall I hit you?"
I said, "Please do"

The gentle tap
Became a break
The blood ran
I began to shake

I clutched a tissue to my nose
Broken trust
In my safe space arose

I wear this break upon my face
A glaring secret
Never discussed
Hidden
Almost no trace

For if we talked
Then you would break
And you are already
Broken

An in my understanding
Of you pain
An in my recognition
Of my own
I know that

I am Healed

Fat and Stupid

One year
Everyday
Fat and Stupid
Fat and Stupid
Fat and Stupid

I believed it for a while
I was just a child
And so were you
My pain inside grew

They say hurt people hurt people
I guess that might be true
But maybe not for you

It's time to let go
Your thoughts don't matter to me
And even if it were true...

What's wrong with being
Fat and Stupid anyway?

Alone

Ostracised
Excluded
Name-called
And bullied

The was no return
From such rejection
I could never
Be your perfection

Only in accepting myself
Was I no longer
Alone

To be at one with who I am

Friendship and absolution came
By finding completion
Alone

Victim

Victim
Is a state of mind
Take the label
And you will find
You will always be
The Victim

Freedom is a state of mind
Take the stance and you will find
You can always be
Free

Twin

A twin died
In our family
When I came to be

Then a twin with me
Is what you thought
You would see

Part of me wonders
If there is still a brother
Missing

Or if all that was lost
Is the hole left
By Mother's grief

I see that within me
There is a him to my her
That forever
I will always be
Whole

Daughter

There is no greater pain I carry
Than knowing
There is no guarantee I will ever
Meet you

To hold a daughter in my arms
To feel a sweet bond of womanhood
To be connected
To all the women before us
And after us

Just know that
If we don't get to meet this time
I will always love you
In this life
And the next

And maybe this time
The only Daughter
I have to nurture is
Me

Depression

It can be so insidious
It can come in the
Being strong
In the shouldering everything

It comes in feeling like there's no space
Always caring for others
Over yourself

And then at some point
It all goes fuzzy
Disconnected from the body
Numb
No longer
Feeling

Joy becomes fleeting
And only exists
In the faces of others

Until somebody asks
Are you OK?
Then you know you have to
Fall apart

Only when Depression is gone
You realise it was there at all

Feeling happiness
Is only possible in the acceptance of
Sadness

And the only way out
Is through

Darkness

So let me unbecome
To let the tears fall
To see my own darkness
The opposing force of joy
To feel everything again
I am no longer scared
Of the Dark

Heart

To think and sense with the
Heart
Is to overcome
The dark voices of the
Head
Bring light into the
Heart, always

We Survived

Earth shattering screams
That clinical smell
Beeps, so many beeps
Pain

So many people
In too small a place
Pain in my belly
Pain down my back
Excruciating
Fever

Too hot
You didn't listen
Until it was clear
That I was very ill
And my son
Urgently
Had to be born

52 hours and drugs
Forceps and cut
Blood on the ceiling
We got him out

I was gray
Blood pressure dangerous
Fever
Not coming down
Sepsis

Stab me with a needle
More drugs
Newborn son
Stab him with a needle
Before I could even
Hold him

We Survived

Son

Son
You came into the world
In such chaos
With stoicism and grace
Eyes wide and wisened
Observing your
New place

Son
I could not believe you were mine
Hours old you sat
Upright on my knee
Your strength was pervading
Your brilliance escaping

Son
Now a child
Every day you amaze
Brilliantly burdened
An amazing mind
In nurturing you
I have found
A sacred place

The Healer

A storm
Disruption
Unplanned
How you appeared
I will never know

Another son
Who changed
Everything

The Healer
Who held me from the inside out
A light when all
Went dark

Who came into this world
With ease and peace
Who eliminated fear
Who loves completely
Whose smile is
Sunshine

Thank you
For letting me
Lose everything

For every bit of change
Only to help me
Discover
Who I really am

You will always be
My Healer

Feeling

As a child
I learned
The answers to
Feeling
Lay at the bottom
Of an alcohol bottle

That feeling was
Weakness
That feeling was
Too difficult
That feeling should be
Numbed
At all costs

You get older
The difficult feelings
Expansive
Anger, acceptable
The bottles grow
Ever deeper

I see your addiction
At 5PM
Hands start to shake

Let's fix feeling
With inebriation

Us
Your children
We will not Numb
We know the only way
To fix feeling is
By feeling

You Took Your Life

First love
How I adored you
In a way you could never
Accept

A darkness
Lay within you
The enemy of joy

As I grew and learned
You pushed me away
How could this light
Ever truly
Love you?

You pushed me away
Rejected
Dejected
Abused
A fell into
A very dark hole

Love came again
To me
In a form of another

So pure
I wished for you
The same

You came back to me
Told of your mistake
Of your love
Too late
I never spoke
To you again

And then one day
I read a message
My heart dropped into
My stomach
You took your life

Part of me was glad
That those memories of us
Only exist in me now
But now I just feel sad

I know you had a life
I know you had love
Of a sort
I am sorry your darkness
Took you away

And know this

That with my pain
And with my empathy
If I can guide others
Back to light
I will

Breathe

Breathe

Pull the air in
Exhale
Let the Fear Out
Inhale
Pull the Light in
Exhale
Let the pain out
Inhale
Pull the love in
Exhale
Let the darkness disperse
Inhale
Feel the earth beneath your feet
Exhale
Feel the tension dissolve

Always

Keep

Breathing

The Witness

I am the Witness
I am Awareness
I let emotion pass through me
The mental chatter I can see
With great clarity
I am Consciousness
I am Spirit
I am Soul
I am what is actually
You

www.ingramcontent.com/pod-product-compliance
Lightning Source LLC
Chambersburg PA
CBHW051755130826
49812CB00033B/1165
* 9 7 8 9 3 5 7 2 1 5 5 5 8 *